Ambrose Weston

A method of increasing the quantity of circulating-money

upon a new and solid principle : letter II

Ambrose Weston

A method of increasing the quantity of circulating-money
upon a new and solid principle ; letter II

ISBN/EAN: 9783744740692

Printed in Europe, USA, Canada, Australia, Japan

Cover: Foto ©Lupo / pixelio.de

More available books at **www.hansebooks.com**

A METHOD

OF

Increasing the Quantity

OF

CIRCULATING-MONEY:

Upon a new and folid Principle.

LETTER II.

ADVERTISEMENT.

———————

.

THE meafure fuggefted in the Firft Letter on this fubject having been approved of by a very great number of thofe who are beft qualified to judge of it,—including perfons of ALL ranks and parties, without diftinction;—I confider it as a tribute of refpect due to thofe who have given their fanction to the general idea of the plan, to fubmit to them the following detail of its propofed practical application, together with anfwers to fome objections :—my defign, in refpect to the diftribution of this Letter, being to limit it, for the prefent, to thofe perfons whofe opinions and fuggeftions upon it, as a fketch ftill admitting of IMPROVEMENT, I am defirous of obtaining.

24th JUNE 1799.

CONTENTS.

SECT.

A

M E T H O D,

&c. &c. &c.

Sᴇᴄᴛ. I.—*Proof of the Necessity of an Extension of the Circulating Medium; which had been before assumed.*

SIR,

Iɴ my former letter upon the subject of my proposal of *a method of increasing the quantity of circulating money*, I assumed the necessity of the measure to be self-evident to those who give attention to the whole circumstances of the case: but, as I find there are *some* who deny the want of an increase of circulating money, I should wish to remind those persons, that they have overlooked several important considerations. It is evident they pay no degree of attention to the impracticability of *borrowing money on* LANDED SECURITY, in consequence as well

of

of the high rate of intereſt obtainable from Government ſecurities, and the expectation of future gain by the riſe of ſtocks, as of the great profits which trade affords; by the operation of which cauſes, the WHOLE circulating capital of the nation is drawn away from land to thoſe more profitable objects; except what is taken up on ANNUITIES,—the moſt pernicious mode of raiſing money, but at this time the *only* expedient by which land-owners can borrow.

THE perſons who maintain that there is at preſent no want of money alſo overlook the poſſibility (*or rather the certainty*) that at ſome period, not very diſtant, TRADE itſelf will again feel that diſtreſs from the obſtructed circulation of money, which occaſioned ſuch extremely ſerious alarm in 1793 and 1796, and the early part of 1797.

I SAY this without ſuppoſing a want of general proſperity in the country: the diſtreſs I allude to may even be cauſed by the increaſe of the commerce of the nation, which poſſibly may yet be doubled; but certainly not without wanting a double capital in money.

THE late ſudden and great increaſe of taxes will alſo require an addition to be made to the circulating medium.—The GOLD withdrawn from circulation muſt alſo be ſupplied by PAPER.

THE

The unusual facility with which money, or Bank-paper, which is *money* whilst it circulates *as such*, has been procureable for some time past by persons of good credit, by way of discount of commercial securities, is chiefly a temporary consequence of the preparation of money to be employed in the Government loan which was eagerly expected during the late winter and spring. We all remember the disappointment of the money-lenders in November last, when Government borrowed only three millions out of fourteen that the loan was expected to consist of. Since that time, no doubt, there has been plenty of money for temporary occasions, but not to lend on mortgages or on personal security, apart from trade. These very opulent persons, who boast of such an abundance of money, will not invest any part of it in purchasing the land-tax, nor in loans to private persons; except in discounting bills or notes for the short period of sixty days, from which there results a greater gain than five per cent. per annum.

Permanent loans, such as are adapted to the slow returns of agriculture, and cannot yield more than the legal rate of interest,—these they utterly decline: and for an obvious reason.— Land-owners have no means of giving more than five per cent. interest,—except by the

destructive

deftructive means of granting *annuities* before taken notice of; but *perfons in trade* feel no difficulty in holding forth to *bankers* the temptation of more than the ftatute-rate of intereft upon loans of money, by means which *cuftom* warrants, and which the *profits* of trade are more than equivalent to.

No perfon who has been much accuftomed to tranfact loans on *mortgages* will deny the want of money, even its entire abfence, in *that* channel of circulation; nor can any perfon who is moderately converfant with what paffes in Weftminfter-Hall be uninformed of the diftrefs which this want of circulation occafions to thofe who, having formerly lent money on land, now want to have it returned, as well as to the unfortunate debtors, who cannot find perfons to affift them in paying off their debts by taking transfers of the exifting mortgages. It is well known to conveyancers that mortgage debts are *moft commonly* difcharged (even when money circulates freely) by transfers to other mortgagees, and not by actual payment on the part of the land-owners, who are *feldom* capable of redeeming their lands : more frequently payment is made by felling the incumbered eftates.

SECT.

WITHOUT something done to assist the LANDED INTEREST, the property in land will change hands almost universally, or to a great extent, within a few years : lands will be brought to sale through the pressure of general distress on the part of the landowners, and the price, which was for some time kept up by peculiar causes, will then fall very low.

IT is beginning to fall already; and I have been well informed that an uncommon proportion *in value* of the estates put up to sale by auction within the last year and more, have been bought in for want of purchasers at a fair price.

IT is high time that the land-owners should begin to look carefully to their own accommodation in respect to the circulation of money; otherwise they must be ruined. This is stating the case without exaggeration; for the merchants are getting vast fortunes, whilst the land-owners are dwindling into comparative insignificance, and are in no small danger of becoming " hewers of " wood and drawers of water" to their rivals, the men of trade.

I SHOULD

I should not state the matter in thefe ftrong terms, if I had not a full conviction that the landed intereft, a very great part of it, is in imminent danger from the circumftances above .fet forth; and if I did not know that ftating the cafe in a cold manner, deftitute of energy, would utterly fail to produce any effect upon that clafs of fociety to which this part of the fubject is peculiarly addreffed.

For there are natural and permanent qualities in the character of the landed gentry of every country which caufe them to give a languid attention to their interefts *as a body*; the indolent and tranquil enjoyment of a revenue coming to them almoft fpontaneoufly, without much thought or any labour, having naturally the effect of indifpofing them to the confideration of danger at a diftance.

Therefore I cannot reafonably expect to be much liftened to by thofe who are moft concerned in what I am now faying, unlefs fome of their own order, or others whofe judgment they are accuftomed to refpect, fhall fupport me in warning them of their danger, and at the fame time recommend the propofed means of relief; or until a nearer approach of the mifchief, with fome feeling of it, fhall awaken their attention.

Sect.

IT has been fuppofed by fome perfons that, becaufe I have, in my former Letter, mentioned *fifty millions or more* as the fum which my fcheme *might* furnifh for the purpofes of circulation, it was my view to have fuch a large fum of money put into circulation whether the occafions of the country required it or not; and upon this miftaken fuppofition they have argued, that a proportionable increafe of the prices of commodities would take place. But I have not propofed any thing like this, though I admit I might have excluded fuch a fuppofition in terms more guarded and lefs liable to be mifunderftood. I did not however fpeak quite incautioufly; for, after mentioning fifty millions or more, I added, " *if* " *fo much could be* EMPLOYED :" and in a former paffage, I had propofed the fcheme to be put in practice upon the ground and within the limits of *neceffity* and *utility*, which I thought a fufficient intimation of the moderate ufe I wifhed to be made of the plan. But even if I had contemplated an immediate iffue of fuch a vaft quantity of paper money, it would not have raifed any fair objection to the principle of the meafure; and indeed the

whole

whole objection is only applicable to the abuse of the plan, and takes for granted that it is to be acted upon without regard to ordinary difcretion.

Sect. IV.—*Prices of Commodities not inconveniently raifed by Paper-Money.*

There are others who have contended, that an inconvenient increafe of the prices of all commodities would take place, if *any* addition were made to the quantity of circulating-money. To this I anfwer as follows:

The increafe of money would not, I think, have the effect of *raifing prices* in refpect to the NECESSARIES of life, becaufe the *quantities* of them (fuppofing the money judicioufly applied by bringing more land into cultivation) would be *increafed* in a greater proportion than the money; yet I do not deny that fuch articles of luxury or curiofity as cannot be increafed in quantity by cultivation or manufacture, would advance in price: but I fuppofe this will not be much infifted upon.

Further, this objection might with equal reafon be urged againft any other meafure which fhould tend gradually to increafe the money of the country; and

and yet such an increase has been at all times, and probably will always continue to be, an object of eager pursuit, notwithstanding the supposed increase of prices consequent thereon.

In fact, a moderate increase of prices is not an evil; for such an increase tends to the extension of agriculture and manufactures, and to stimulate industry in every possible way, and therefore is a great benefit to a country by augmenting the quantity of its commodities; and this, by its reaction, prevents the rise of prices from being too rapidly accelerated.

Even high prices are only disadvantageous when they are occasioned by a permanent, or an extreme scarcity of commodities, or a very sudden scarcity, that is, when the demand continues for a long time, or in a very uncommon degree, or suddenly happens to exceed the supply; and, in general, a period of high prices is soon followed by abundance, and sometimes by extraordinary cheapness; the high price operating as an incitement to produce new and greater quantities of the commodity which yields an unusual profit.

Add to which, that the rise of prices is, in a great degree, an imaginary evil, so far as adding to the stock of money may be supposed to occasion the increase increafe of prices; for, in general, every man's fhare of money would be increafed too. The price of labour would rife as well as other things; and this joint increafe would caufe new exertions of diligence, by inciting or obliging many perfons to work who are now idle, or to work with greater diligence than before.

I EXCEPT, however, the cafe of perfons who live on fixed incomes, which they are incapable of enlarging. To them, every increafe of prices cannot but be a difadvantage. It is an unavoidable inconvenience, necefarily attendant upon the ftationary pofition they hold. But it is not to be expecreated that the general progrefs of fociety is to be retarded, in order that thefe perfons may feel no manner of inconvenience from the circumftances which keep them in a ftate of inactivity, or hinder them from bettering their fortunes. The vigour of the nation cannot be kept down to the *par* of their imbecility; nor would this finally be any benefit to them, but very much the contrary: even if all neighbouring countries fhould, by univerfal agreement, confent to be ftationary too,— ceafing their progreffion in the arts and enjoyments of life. However, in the end, even perfons thus circumftanced would,—I mean *many* of them, —derive advantage from the operation of the plan,

by

by partaking, from collateral and accidental caufes, in the general profperity; and *all* of them would be eafed by the reduction of taxes, which would be one of the moft probable and moft extenfive confequences of the propofed meafure, as more fully noticed in a fubfequent part of this Letter.

Sect. V.—*The Advantages of the Plan, how to be difpofed of.*

It has been faid, I underftand, by fome perfons, that there is a *partiality* in giving to the ftockholders the great advantages I have fpoken of.

I have faid the emoluments to refult from the plan ought to be divided between the Stock-Proprietors, the Bank of England, and the Government, (that is, the nation at large,) in fuch proportions as may be agreed upon; of courfe, in juft and equitable proportions. Surely *fome* fhare of the advantages muft be given to the ftock-transferrers, and fufficient to induce them to engage their property in the execution of the fcheme. This is all that I have in view, or have fuggefted.

And this may be done in the following manner:—Let the privilege of iffuing the propofed notes

c   be

be given to the Subfcribers to FUTURE GOVERN-
MENT LOANS: and as the Subfcribers, with
this *bonus* given to them, would take the loans on
better terms, in proportion to the advantages they
obtained, *the whole Public* would by that means
largely participate in the profit to refult from the
fcheme.

SECT. VI.—*How the Plan may be applied to the Relief of the Landed Interefl.*

MY defign from the beginning was, and ftill is,
to accomplifh, if I am able, the procuring of
afliftance to thofe who want money upon the fecurity of land to enable them to pay their debts, or
to improve their eftates; and even this not for
their fakes only, but for the general good of the
country.

IF the fcheme I have propofed fhould take a
more extenfive range, and become applicable to
other purpofes befides the relief of the landed
intereft, it will be an accidental refult. I was
looking for one thing, and it may turn out that I
have found another of more importance; or rather
an application of what I had in view to a more
important fubjeft. I believe this is what commonly happens in fuch cafes.

BUT

But (in relation to the landed interest), I think the plan in question may be adapted to the accommodation of the LAND PROPRIETORS in the following manner:

LET the persons who are to obtain the notes upon the security of their transferred stock engage to lend the notes upon MORTGAGES of LAND, and to deposit the mortgages in the Bank of England within a limited time; their transferred stock being a security for the performance of this engagement. And let the Mortgages, when deposited, be declared by the act of the Legislature, which is to establish the whole measure, a further and collateral security for the amount of the circulating notes;— each mortgage for the amount of the notes lent thereon. Thus the note-creditor, however well satisfied he might be with the original security of the stock, would have another security of probably twice the amount of the notes,—a security far superior to that of an undefined, and, in some measure one may say, an imaginary quantity of gold deposited in a Bank. Every million of notes would be represented by four millions of stock and about two millions sterling in land!—I do not, however, mean to represent this ADDITIONAL security as NECESSARY to give strength to the original plan. I propose it as

subordinate

fubordinate and convenient merely, not at all as being effential.

THE mortgages when depofited would be capable of being transferred like other mortgages, but always fubject to a general LIEN for the amount of the notes lent thereon; and might be difcharged by bringing in to be cancelled an equal amount in notes of the fame kind; thefe being cancelled, (that is, an equal amount, not the identical notes lent upon each mortgage,) the land might be reconveyed to the proper owner for the time being, difcharged of the mortgage. And, at the fame time, the transferred ftock connected with the mortgage fo releafed, might be re-transferred to the perfon to whom it fhould then belong.

BY this means there would be a conftant tendency of fome portion of the notes to return into the Bank to be cancelled; which would prevent an exceffive accumulation of the quantity : fome periods might alfo be fixed for this purpofe, and with this view; whereby the gradual and final extinction of the notes might be provided for, if a change of circumftances fhould require fuch extinction,

THIS operation of lending upon mortgages fhould be left, I think, to the difcretion of the

INDI-

INDIVIDUALS by whom the loans are made, both in respect to the titles to the mortgaged lands, and the quantity of security, and, within some limits to be prescribed, the periods of repayment also; except that some superintendence would be proper merely to ascertain that the loans were made bonâ fide upon the lands appearing in the several mortgages, and not employed for any other purpose in the first instance.—Of which the deposit of the mortgages, with proper inspection, would furnish good evidence.

THE risk of the security would upon this footing rest upon each individual lender; but that risk, after the plan shall have been acted upon for some considerable time, would be much less than it is now in similar loans; because, as by the means proposed there would be established a very extensive *register of mortgages*, the disputes and frauds which too often attend securities of that nature would to a great degree be avoided.

THIS restriction of the loans (so long as it should be thought right to continue such restriction) to landed securities would in itself limit the quantity of the proposed notes to the amount of the demand of money by land-owners desirous of borrowing. From them the money would be absorbed into the general

general circulation, by payment of their debts, and by their making agricultural and other improvements.—By this means, alſo, tradeſmen who are diſtreſſed for want of more early payment than they now receive, would be enabled to carry on their buſineſs and make their own payments with greater facility and more comfort than they can do at preſent.

SECT. VII.—*General Advantages.*

THUS, PUBLIC INDUSTRY would receive a new impulſe, employment would be given to many who are now in want of it, lands now unimproved and waſte would be brought into cultivation, houſes and other buildings would be repaired or erected, canals would be completed that are now left unfiniſhed for want of money, bridges would be built, mines would be worked, NEW SOURCES of trade would be opened, and COMMERCE in a thouſand ways would be invigorated and put into a ſtate of activity.

THIS may ſeem to ſuppoſe a more free uſe of the propoſed money than could probably take place through loans on land only ; but in whatever way, or to whatever extent, the money ſhould be employed, the maſs and quantity of uſeful and neceſſary commodities,

commodities, and confequently the comforts of the people, would be increafed by this additional ftimulus given to the national exertion. This increafe would be proportionably greater than the increafe of money, fuppofing the latter to be added to with difcretion and by flow and gentle degrees, and not by an inundation of new reprefentative-figns ; for it muft all along be borne in mind, that PUBLIC WISDOM is to direct the operation and to be employed in controlling the tides of this new money.

SECT. VIII.—*Effect of the Plan upon the Rate of Intereft, and Reduction of the National Debt.*

ONE of the moft direct confequences to be expected from my plan, is the lowering of the RATE OF INTEREST. If it fhould be reduced generally below five per cent. that reduction would take away a part of the gain originally computed in the plan. But this would be counterbalanced by the good effects which a low rate of intereft always produces, and by other beneficial confequences which the plan may be made to accomplifh.

INDEED, this lowering of the rate of intereft would be, above all other means, I conceive, the

beft

beſt auxiliary to the fund eſtabliſhed by Parliament for relieving the nation from the preſſure of its GREAT DEBT.

A MOST happy event it would be, if the five per cent. ſtock could be reduced to four, and the other ſtocks in like proportion. A reduction to that extent would be the ſame thing in ſubſtance as a gratuitous extinction of a FIFTH PART of the NATIONAL DEBT; which conſiſts altogether, in reſpect to the right of demanding payment, in the ANNUITY payable by the nation to its creditors. Nor would it be difficult to effect a reduction to this amount by the help of the plan in queſtion; ſuppoſing the funds ſhall ever again come to the prices they were at in 1792; a ſuppoſition which this plan would alſo tend to realize. I admit that this reduction can only accompany the fall of the market-rate of intereſt.

THIS operation of diminiſhing the annual outgoing might begin preciſely at the period when the SINKING FUND would loſe part of its beneficial efficacy, in reſpect to buying up the public debt, on account of the near approach of 3 per cent. ſtock to par; in which ſtock purchaſes could then no longer be made with advantage, till the whole of the 5 per cent. and 4 per cent. ſtocks ſhould be
bought

bought up. And though the latter flocks would be above par, the public would derive no gain from that circumftance, though the flock-holder might feem to fuftain a lofs by having his ftock paid off at par. But the near profpect of fuch an event would keep thofe flocks from attaining the prices they would otherwife reach.

As, at the period I am now fpeaking of, the annual produce of the SINKING FUND could not, for the foregoing reafons, be applied with great advantage in buying up the national debt, I fubmit it might then be better difpofed of, as a PREMIUM, in conjunction with the PRIVILEGE of iffuing the notes in queftion, towards inducing monied men to lend large fums of money at a rate below the then current rate of intereft to be applied in paying off at par thofe debts which now carry a HIGH intereft. It will be foon found that I am not fpeaking without confideration when I talk of borrowing *below* the current rate of intereft, if that is not apparent already.

IN this way, though the *nominal* amount of the debt might continue to be the fame as before, ftill the nation would be relieved by the reduction of the *annuity* in which the debt fubftantially confifts; and TAXES might then be repealed to a proportion-

D   able

able amount, or the SINKING FUND might be enlarged, fuppofing the whole taxes to be fuftained fome time longer: or, the *faving* might be applied in part to each of thefe objects.

To explain this propofed operation by an example:—Let us imagine an eftate to be incumbered with a debt of £. 100,000, at 5 per cent. intereft, or £. 5000 per annum. Then conceive the owner to be poffeffed of £. 10,000 in ready money, which if applied towards payment of the debt would reduce it to £. 90,000, and the annual intereft to £. 4500. But the owner, having regard as well to his own future convenience as to that of his family after him, is defirous that his eftate fhould be liable to a lefs annual outgoing; and therefore propofes *to give the ten thoufand pounds* of which he is poffeffed, *as a premium* to induce fome perfon to pay off the debt on the eftate, and to accept a transfer of the fecurity at a lower rate than 5 per cent. And, in order further to abate the intereft, he offers to give to the lender fome *extremely valuable privileges* of which he may be fuppofed to have the command. Add to this an expectation then formed, that the current rate of intereft will fpeedily fall below 4 per cent. by the operation of fome known caufes.

UNDER

UNDER thefe circumftances, we may fuppofe that the new lender would advance his money at a lower rate than 5, or even than 4 per cent.—Grant it might be 3 per cent.—And if this fhould be the cafe, the annual incumbrance on the eftate will be reduced from £. 5000 to £. 3000.

I THINK the analogy is fo plain, that it is hardly neceffary to add that the £. 10,000 reprefents the produce of the *Sinking Fund* for a fhort period, fuppofe two or three years (more or lefs); and the *privileges* hinted at are correlative to the iffuing of notes to circulate as money on the credit of ftock.—The reft is quite obvious.

SUPPOSING this to be underftood and affented to, I may now go on to fay, that if, at the period above alluded to, the produce of the INCOME TAX fhould be applied in the fame manner towards the reduction of the rate of intereft, the *effect* produced in that way would be *greater*, and the *tax itfelf* might properly be made to ceafe *fooner*, than by its application towards extinguifhing the capital of the public debt.

AND in this refpect, as well as in the general tendency of the plan to produce an abatement of

taxes,

taxes, perfons of fixed incomes would have the fatisfaction of feeing their own advantage connected with the public welfare; a circumftance which I have before alluded to, and which I have great pleafure in thus explaining and confirming : for I am anxious that my propofal fhould produce nothing but GOOD ; if that CAN be.

I ALLOW, that fo far as the produce of the *Sinking Fund* and that of the *Income Tax* are called in aid of this reduction of the annuity, the reduction would not be *gratuitous* ; it is true :—but this does not hinder my firft fuggeftion on this point from being alfo true, namely, that the reduction in queftion might be brought about merely and folely by the help of this plan.—I believe it *might,* confidering the *command over the rate of intereft* which it would give to thofe who hold the reins of government: a moft important CONTROL *in the hands of thofe who are to manage on the part of the* DEBTOR !

YET it ftill may be proper to make the Sinking Fund and Income Tax co-operate to the fame end ; by which means a greater and more fpeedy effect will be produced towards leffening the national debt, than could be managed by the unaffifted operation of this plan.

THERE

THERE certainly is not any thing that can fo ef-
fectually promote this reduction of the annual outgoing, as keeping the circulation of money conftantly full, and by that means lowering the rate of
intereft; which hitherto there has not exifted the
means of doing, but which by a right ufe of my
plan may be accomplifhed: and this makes it be,
what I humbly conceive it is,—*a great political en-
gine*; in a word, A NEW POWER. I cannot refrain
from faying *fo much*; for either it is THAT, or it is
NOTHING.

SECT. IX.—*Bank of England.—How this Plan may be connected with it.*

IT appears from the evidence before the SECRET
COMMITTEE on BANK AFFAIRS, that there were
times within the ten years which preceded the
Bank's ceafing to make payments in cafh, when
the directors *deliberated* on reducing the rate of dif-
count: but they never did it; and though the reafons why they did not are left to be conjectured, it
appears to me moft clear that one of the principal
caufes which hindered the eftablifhment of that fa-
lutary regulation, was an uncertainty on the part of
the Bank, whether they could conftantly keep the
circulation full, or whether they might venture to

encourage

encourage the abundant circulation which a low rate of intereſt would tend to promote.

How ſoon, under the preſent circumſtances, the Bank may again think fit to leſſen the amount of their *diſcounts*, I do not pretend to conjecture ; but ſome conſiderable effect in that way might probably be produced by a repeal of the preſent reſtriction on the iſſue of *caſh*.

I NOW come to ſhew how my plan may be connected with the eſtabliſhment of the BANK of ENGLAND.

I SUBMIT that THAT BANK, though it has peculiar intereſts of its own, may be moulded to purpoſes of public utility within the limits of a juſt and reaſonable regard to thoſe its intereſts. It OUGHT NOT to ſtand in the way of the general good of the community.

THEREFORE, with due regard to the Bank intereſts, I go on to ſay that there ought to be a PROPORTION between the Bank capital and effects, and the amount of the notes circulated on the credit thereof.

I PRESUME to ſuggeſt, that THAT PROPORTION ſhould be publicly *known* and *regulated by law*.

This

This *publicity* would at all times protect the Bank against a *run* upon it, which can only proceed from panic fears and a distrust of its security, occasioned by ignorance of its actual situation.

THE amount of the circulating notes of the Bank, that is to say, *circulating on the credit of the Bank capital,* ought never to exceed a *fixed* sum; let us suppose twelve millions.

ALL circulating bank paper *beyond* that amount ought to rest on other security.

Now to apply these principles; let the Bank issue its own notes instead of the notes I have called stock-notes. Let there be no distinction.

BUT let the Bank be *permanently protected* by law against paying CASH beyond the amount of its own proper or restricted quantity of notes—*its own debt*—the twelve millions above mentioned.

Now suppose twenty millions to be in circulation, or any given sum exceeding twelve millions, the Bank might be liable (supposing the present restriction taken off) to be called upon for *cash* to the amount of twelve millions; — but the surplus sum they could not be required to pay in cash;

cash; therefore they could not say their own establish-
ment was endangered by the additional quantity of
notes circulated on the credit of stock.

But if twenty millions were in circulation, the general call on the Bank for cash may be supposed to
be proportionably greater than if only twelve millions
circulated; therefore the Bank must keep a greater
proportion of gold in their treasury to carry on its
business; and for this, as well as for the management of the additional issue of notes, the Bank
should receive a compensation, including a reason-
able profit.—I shall for the present rest the matter
here so far as concerns the Bank, conceiving that
all its essential interests are thus fully taken care of.

Sect. X.—*The Security and Convenience to the Public under this Plan.*

In respect to the Public, I cannot discover any
objection that they can make to the increased circulation of bank notes upon the principles now
laid down. They have been content with an almost
total restriction of the issue of gold in payment of
bank notes, and why should they not be equally
well content with having a moderate proportion of
those notes permanently exempted from being

paid

paid in cafh, there being other and moft abundant fecurity for their amount ?—To fuppofe any inconvenience, one muft make a previous fuppofition that all the notes of the Bank of England, circulating upon the credit of their own capital, are required to be paid in cafh, with a fettled purpofe not to let it return there. But this fuppofes the natural death of the Bank; a perpetual ceffation of its ufe as a bank: a moft chimerical · fuppofition! But even granting this infinitely improbable event to take place, ftill the furplus quantity of notes would be reprefented by a fourfold quantity of ftock and a double value in land, and thefe remaining notes would then be more convenient and neceffary than ever: for the Bank of England notes, its own proper and reftricted quantity, being fuppofed extinguifhed, the furplus notes would be effentially neceffary to the purpofes of COMMERCE, if any were fuppofed to remain.

THESE NOTES WOULD THEREFORE CONTINUE TO CIRCULATE; and by fuitable provifions to be made by the Legiflature at that time, might be liquidated in gold and filver as occafion might require. To fuppofe the contrary, is to fuppofe trade annihilated and all occafions for remittances from place to place within Great Britain to be put an end to for ever. So that it is only by imagining feveral events to take place, each of them involving, if not contradictions, at

E   leaft

leaft very high degrees of improbability, that the circulation of the propofed notes once begun can be expected ever to ceafe.

THE fuppofition of the extinction of that quantity of notes which is peculiarly to belong to the Bank of England, I need hardly fay is made by way of argument, and not' with any expectation of its ever being realized. But the very putting of fuch a cafe, even in this way, may appear alarming to fome; therefore, I might propofe that the whole profits to refult from the new quantity of notes fhould be, annually or half yearly, fubjected in the firft place to indemnify the Bank of England againft fuch lofs or detriment as this fcheme may bring upon them; that indemnity being made good out of the dividends of the tranferred ftock. I believe fuch a guarantee (under circumftances fo very improbable) from the new fyftem to the old one, would not deprive the former, the new fyftem, of any part of its efficacy, or caufe the ftock-proprietors to abate their expectations of gain from the operation of the fcheme. The effect of fuch arrangement would be, that the Bank of England would have conftantly a profit upon twelve millions, or whatever might be the reftricted or the actual amount of their circulation, not exceeding twelve millions;

and

and the ſtock-transferers would have the profit upon whatever might at any time be the additional quantity; ſubject, in reſpect to the latter, to a proper deduction out of the dividends of the transferred ſtock for the charges of management and otherwiſe in favour of the Bank.—I believe this will appear eaſily intelligible to thoſe who will take the trouble of thinking a little upon the point: but I am ſenſible this part of the caſe requires rather more attention than the reſt.—It is, however, of the leaſt conſequence, as it applies only to the moſt improbable of all the ſuppoſitions which the caſe requires to be made: and if it creates a difficulty in the mind of any reader, it may be paſſed over, without any diſadvantage to the right comprehenſion of the ſcheme: for it is only an anſwer to a very refined and even imaginary objection.

Sect. XI.—*The Queſtions re-ſtated.*

But, the original queſtion recurs:—Is there a *want* of circulating-money? And alſo the other queſtion, —Will the *Public* receive and circulate *theſe* notes *as caſh?*—Concerning both of which queſtions, if I expreſſed naturally and without reſerve all that I think and feel, I ſhould manifeſt ſuch a degree of

confidence

confidence of having made good what I have had in view, as would fcarcely feem confiftent with that deference with which I mean, Sir, to fubmit the whole matter to your fuperior difcernment; as I muft ultimately do to the JUDGMENT of the Public.

SECT. XII.—*Some particular Objections ftated.*

To the PUBLIC, therefore, I fubmit *all* that I have faid, *together alfo* with the *following objections,* which, having been communicated to me, I thus make known, becaufe I have already faid, in the introduction to my Firft Letter, that I will difguife nothing. Indeed, it would be quite ufelefs to hide any fubftantial objection, or to fuppofe that any defects in my fcheme would efcape the clear-fighted judgment of thofe who are to decide upon it.

OBJECTIONS.

1. THE national debt is the wealth of indivi-duals; but it is wealth already employed by the ftate, and *not applicable to the pur-pofes of commerce.*

2. THERE

2. THERE is a miftake in thinking, that perfons who take bank-notes would take ftock-notes. The former are grounded on a very different fecurity from the other; as their circulation is occafioned by a BELIEF that the Bank is poffeffed of *fpecie* to anfwer the payment of its notes when called upon.

3. THE plan makes every ftockholder a banker, iffuing notes WITHOUT FUNDS, or precious metals, to anfwer them.

4. THE ftock-notes would not, as reprefented in the plan, be a mortgage on the induftry of the nation, but on the inactive capital of individuals and the debts of GOVERNMENT.

5. IT is faid, " the wealth in the funds is dead " and unproductive;" *fo it muft* with refpect to the proprietor; for it cannot be applied to *two* purpofes.

6. IT is faid, that a want of money or a reprefentative fign fhould not be known to thofe who poffefs property or credits well fecured. But can they have *both* the *property* and its *reprefentative* ?

SECT.

Sect. XIII.—*Replies to thofe Objections, and Conclufion.*

I do not mean much to lengthen this Letter by replies to thefe objections : for I fhould think I had employed my time to little purpofe in all the foregoing remarks, and fhould appear to have little confidence in the difcernment of thofe who will read this and my former Letter,—as well as much diftruft of the candour and opennefs to conviction of the perfon who made the objections,—if I were now to fpend any confiderable portion of time in pointing out how completely I have obviated *all* thefe objections. But, without defigning to imitate the almoft oracular concifenefs of the objections, I think it may be proper for me to fay a few words in anfwer thereto.

The firft objection begs the queftion.—It admits the national debt to be the wealth of individuals; but adds, that it is wealth already employed by the State, *and not applicable to the purpofes of commerce.* No reafon, however, is affigned for this affertion. On the contrary, I have given reafons for thinking, that *fome part* of this *acknowledged* wealth of individuals *may* be applied to purpofes of commerce. I have heard the objection ftated

in

in *this* manner :—" The wealth in the funds is
" MONEY SPENT." But I fay, NO ; it is not *money
fpent :* it is, WITH RESPECT TO THE CREDITOR,
MONEY LENT ; and it is BY the creditor that I propofe it to be now employed, by mortgaging his fecurity. The objector did not perceive that his pofition, *that this is* MONEY SPENT, is only true in
relation to the STATE, by whom it is not *now* to be
employed, but, as before obferved, by its creditors.
And why may not this be ?—Compare it with any
other mortgage, and it will appear that it *may* pro-
cure *credit*, and be the means of *circulation*, in favour of the *mortgagee.*

THE fecond objection alfo begs the queftion ;
and ftates incorrectly the ground upon which
bank notes circulate, which is *not a* BELIEF
*that the Bank is poffeffed of fpecie to anfwer the
payment of its notes when called upon*; or, if fuch
a belief were the ground of that circulation, it would
be a belief that delights in evident improbabilities
and detected errors.

Do we not all of us KNOW, that on the 27th of
February 1797, the Bank of England was *not* poffeffed of fpecie to anfwer its notes when called
upon ? Do we not alfo know, that from that period to the prefent we have not been able to obtain
from

from the Bank of England either gold or filver for a ten pound bank note ? Yet this did not, even in February 1797, when the panic was at its height, hinder the free circulation of bank notes ; which circulation is *not* founded on the *belief* which the objection fuppofes, but on *other and ftronger grounds*, too obvious to need pointing out.

THE third objection afferts what is quite a miftake in point of *fact*, in faying that the propofed notes would be iffued " *without funds* ;" unlefs it be true that the property of the Bank of England in three per cent. confolidated Bank annuities is *not a fund* for the fecurity of its own notes.

THE fourth objection is inconfiftent with the third, in reprefenting *that* to be inactive *capital*, which before had been defcribed as *no fund*. This objection alfo quotes imperfectly what I have faid, which was, that the fecurity upon which the notes are to circulate would be a FIRST MORTGAGE on the PROPERTY and INDUSTRY of the nation ; *and this I re-affert.* Why does the objection drop the *pro-perty* of the nation as a part of the fecurity ; and why call the *national* funds the *debts* of GOVERN-MENT, when they are the debts of the WHOLE COUNTRY ?

DEBTS not funded may be called government debts. These, if contracted without parliamentary authority, the nation may decline to fanction and adopt: but when once funds are provided to fecure them, by authority of the LEGISLATURE, the debts become from thenceforth *debts of the nation,* and are fecured upon the land, the money, the goods, the commerce, and the induftry of the country; and, with all thefe, the PUBLIC FAITH is pledged to the creditors.

THE fifth objection again begs the queftion; for I have fhewn how the wealth in the funds *may* be applied to *two* purpofes; if the principles which I have endeavoured to eftablifh by *argument,* and not by mere affertion, are found to be valid.

To the fixth objection I anfwer, that thofe who poffefs property of any kind may poffefs that property in a *mortgaged ftate,* and alfo at the fame time a reprefentative fign *to the extent of the mortgage.*

FOR the fake of brevity, and for other reafons, I have omitted fome things that might be faid in confirmation of my pofitions, and perhaps even fome explanations that may be thought neceffary by thofe who are fond of minute ftatements; but I

think

think it beſt to leave the matter here.—Permit me,
therefore, to conclude with what I cannot but think
very honourable to myſelf—I mean, a declaration
of the ſincere and reſpectful attachment with which
I am bound ever to be,

SIR,

Your devoted and faithful ſervant,

&c. &c. &c.